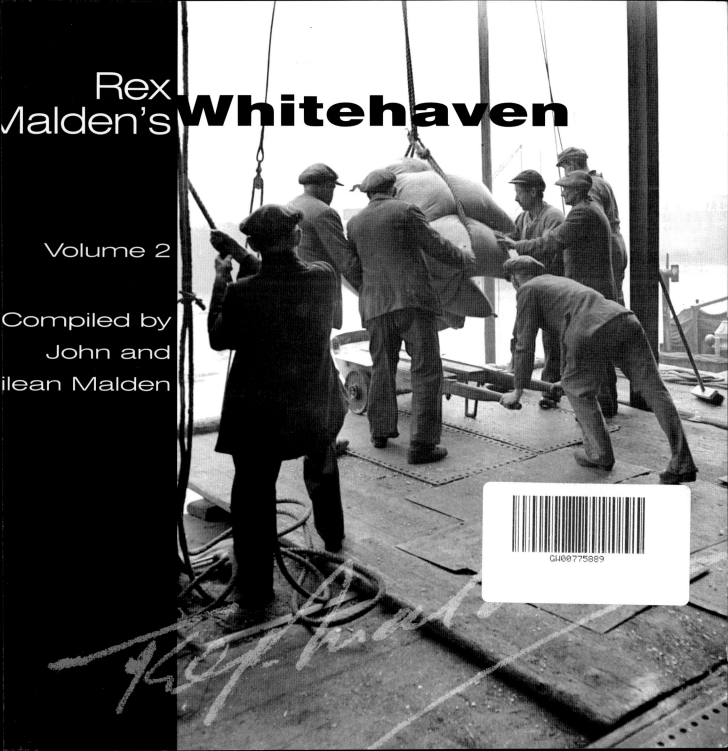

Rex Malden's **Whitehaven**

Volume 2

Compiled by
John and
Eilean Malden

First published in Great Britain in 2001 by Try Malden Limited.

ISBN 0-9539257-1-4

For more information, or to place orders for other publications or prints you should contact:
Try Malden Limited,
5, Greenlaw Avenue,
Paisley,
Renfrewshire PA1 3RB
Tel: 0141-889-4302
E mail: try.malden@virgin.net

Designed by: Key Design and Print
Printed by: The James McVicar Printing Works
Distributed by: Try Malden Limited

Also in this series:
Whitehaven Volume 1
Wigton Volume 1

We were quite over-whelmed when the first volume in this series won the Border Television Award for Best Illustrated Book, together with the overall Lakeland Book of the Year Award for 2001.

As a child, I was allowed to practice various photo-graphic skills in my father's darkroom in Corbridge Vicarage. By that time, the mid 1950's, he had almost abandoned his beloved hobby of black & white photography due to pressure of parish work, and only took a few colour transparencies during family holidays. In an atmosphere of fixer & developer smells - crocodile's breath - as my mother called it, my elder brother and I experimented with outdated chemicals and paper under my father's tuition. I knew that he had won prizes in photographic competitions, kept scrap books of contact prints and files containing some 4,500 negatives, but never realised, until comparatively recently, what an excellent photographer he had been. Added to this, he kept

a meticulous record of every photograph taken, including time, place, speed, f stop &c.

My father, Reginald Giles Malden, always known as Rex, was born in London on 8th April 1899. A son and grandson of the Vicarage, his interest in photography started in his teens and was encouraged by his father and grandfather's interest in the medium. When he left King Edward's School, Canterbury towards the end of the First World War, he enlisted in the Bedfordshire Regiment, only to be told that he had a weak heart. He was put on light duties, including guarding a prisoner of war camp. During his brief time in the army, he started smoking, remaining a heavy smoker into his seventies, and received his vocational call to enter the Church.

When he left the army, my father went up to Trinity College, Cambridge, to read Classics. Being small of stature, he was chosen to cox the 1st & 3rd Trinity crew. After graduating, he attended Ely Theological College and was ordained deacon in

1923 and priest in the following year. Whilst at Cambridge he had come into contact with Rt Rev'd Philip Crick, who had recently been appointed as Bishop of Rockhampton in Queensland, Australia. Crick was intent on reviving the Bush Brotherhood. He invited my father and one of his colleagues, Leonard Poole, to join him in Australia following their ordinations. After a brief period serving as Curate at St.Luke's, Gillingham, Kent, my father set sail for Australia with Poole and two members of the choir, John Bloom and Bill Alp. During the two years he spent in Australia, his interest in photography grew, and he brought back some sixty negatives of people and places around Barcaldine and Long Reach in Queensland. These negatives have now been deposited with the Barcaldine Local History Society and copies kept in the Queensland State archives.

On his return, my father was appointed Curate of St.Nicholas, Brighton, where he married Margaret Grace (Meg) Reynolds, on 22nd June 1928. My sister Anne was born there. The young couple and small baby moved to Whitehaven in January 1931. The move must have been a considerable culture shock for them. My father had been brought up very High Church, and had lived most of his life in rural Cambridgeshire. They were moving from the affluent suburbia of Sussex to a Cumberland coal mining town where my father spent his first week burying the dead from the Haig Pit disaster.

My parents soon adapted, and grew to love the north of England, the home of my mother's Quaker ancestors. With the birth of my sister Mary and the addition of a long suffering black labrador called Paddy, my father's photographic interest became a passionate hobby. Always experimenting, he found a wealth of subjects to record and had the great gift of being able to compose and take a shot without having to repeat it.

The photographs in this volume have been chosen to evoke the life and times of the people of Whitehaven in the 1930's. We let the photographs speak for themselves and leave the telling of the shipbuilding and mining history of the Town to those far better qualified.

My parents left Whitehaven in February 1941, and moved north to the small market town of Wigton. Here the family expanded to include my brother and myself. During the winter of 1947 we moved to Corbridge in Northumberland, where my father acted as Rural Dean and was made a Canon of Newcastle Cathedral. He retired in 1970 and my parents moved firstly to Alnwick and then to York, where he died on 2nd January 1982.

John Malden

31st March 1938
The William Pit, one of eight pits in the immediate vacinity of Whitehaven
[3.30pm f8 1/100]

29th August 1939
The Wellington Pit
[12 noon f5.6 1/100]

9th April 1938
The William Pit shift waiting to go down beside the inclined railway
[9.30am f11 $1/50$]

27th September 1939
The Haig Pit engine
[5.30pm f2.9 1/5]

21st May 1938
Coal trucks beside Pattinson's Mill, waiting to be unloaded
[11.20am f8 $^1/_{50}$]

31st March 1938
My father's famous
photograph of
Mary Ellen Spence
carrying coal in front
of the William Pit.
She is wearing the
traditional steel-toed
wooden clogs
[3.30pm f8 ¹/₁₀₀]

1935
A hastily taken snap of Ruth Currie and Florrie Weighman. They collected 'crackers' – sea washed coal from Salton Beach to earn a living. They had to carry the bags from door to door until someone bought the coal. We include this photograph as a reminder of how hard times could be.

27th May 1938
The Coaster Ausma being loaded with coal
[12.30pm f11 1¹/₁₀₀]

29th May 1939
Boats at the loader, with Pattinson's Mill in the background. The coal
loader on the right of the picture has been hoisted up out of the way.
[10am f4 $^{1}/_{100}$]

7th April 1938
The conveyor belt
loader lowered over
the hold of a coaster
[12.30pm f4 1/250]

7th April 1938
The dust created by loading coal by conveyor.
For obvious reasons, some boats only carried 'dirty' cargo!
[12.30pm f4 1/250]

1933
A Timber boat being unloaded by steam driven cranes

19th May 1938
A Timber boat, with the Grand Hotel in the background.
The steam crane on the left waits to start the unloading.
[5pm f11 1/100]

20th May 1938
Unloading the Timber
boat at the fitting
out berth
[10am f11 $^{1}/_{100}$]

21st May 1939
The steam crane loading timber trucks.
The Grand Hotel in the background stood on the site of the present Tesco store.
[11.30am f8 $1/50$]

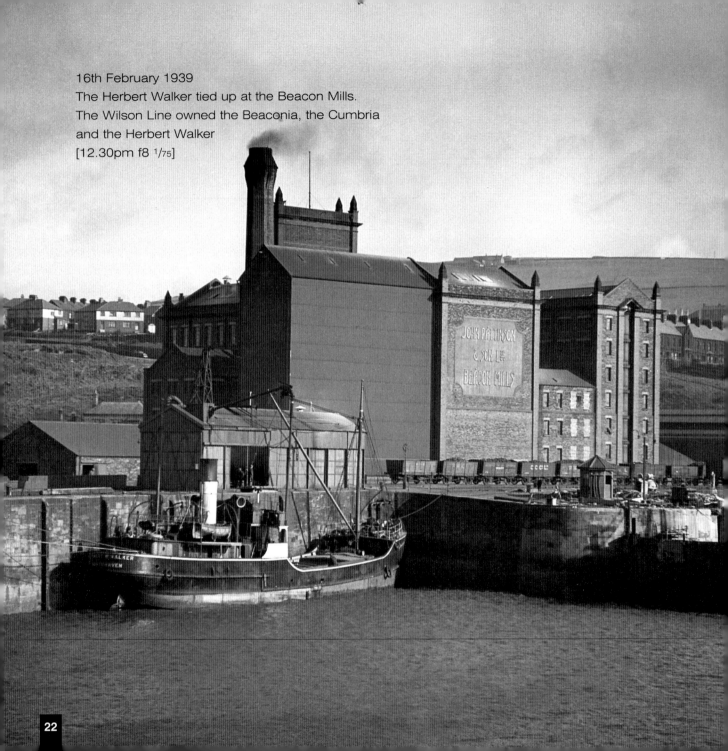

16th February 1939
The Herbert Walker tied up at the Beacon Mills.
The Wilson Line owned the Beaconia, the Cumbria
and the Herbert Walker
[12.30pm f8 1/75]

July 1938
Unloading
grain with the
vacuum lift
from the hold
of a coaster
[4pm f4 1/250]

31st March 1938
Mixed cargo in
the hold of
Herbert Walker.
It was known as
the bread and
butter boat,
plying between
Whitehaven and
Liverpool.
The boat has
grounded at
low tide.
[3.30pm f5.6 $^{1}/_{100}$]

31st March 1938
Unloading the
Herbert Walker with
Alf Tugman on the
left and Tom Finlay
on the right
[3.30pm f8 $^{1}/_{50}$]

31st March 1938
Unloading the Herbert
Walker. One man
sits on the barrow
handle to stop it
tipping up as the
barrels are lowered
[3.30pm f5.6 1/100]

29th May 1939
The Hold of the
Herbert Walker.
The mouth of the hold
was covered with
boards and tarpaulins
during the voyage.
[10am f2.9 1/25]

May 1938
A small crane at work
on repairs to the dock
[10am f5.6 ¹/₅₀]

20th May 1938
Painting the ship
[10am f8 $1/50$]

5th February 1938
Swans at the harbour
[12 noon f3.5 $^{1}/_{100}$]

The North pier on a stormy day, looking towards Lowca

March 1938
Swans at Limc Tonguc
[11.45am f10 1/100]

28th January 1939
My sisters Anne & Mary on Golden Sands
[12.45pm $1/5$ f8]

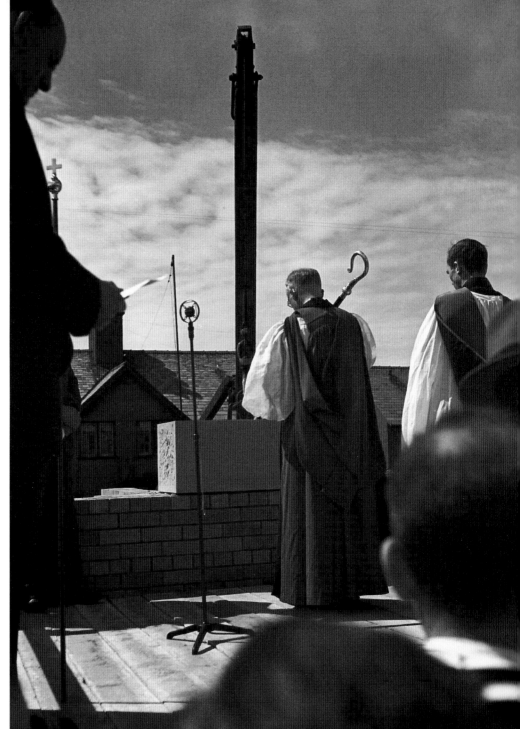

2nd July 1938
Laying the foundation
stone for St. Peter's
Church, Kells, by the
Bishop of Carlisle.
A microphone stands
to his left.
[3.30pm f8 $^{1}/_{100}$]

27th January 1938
The Building nearing completion
[11.30am f5.6 1/50]

28th November 1939
The completed building. The Church was consecrated 16th September 1939
[9.30am f5.6 $^{1}/_{50}$]

18th September 1939
Looking east from Gallery, South aisle St.Peter's, Kells
[12 noon f16 12 secs]

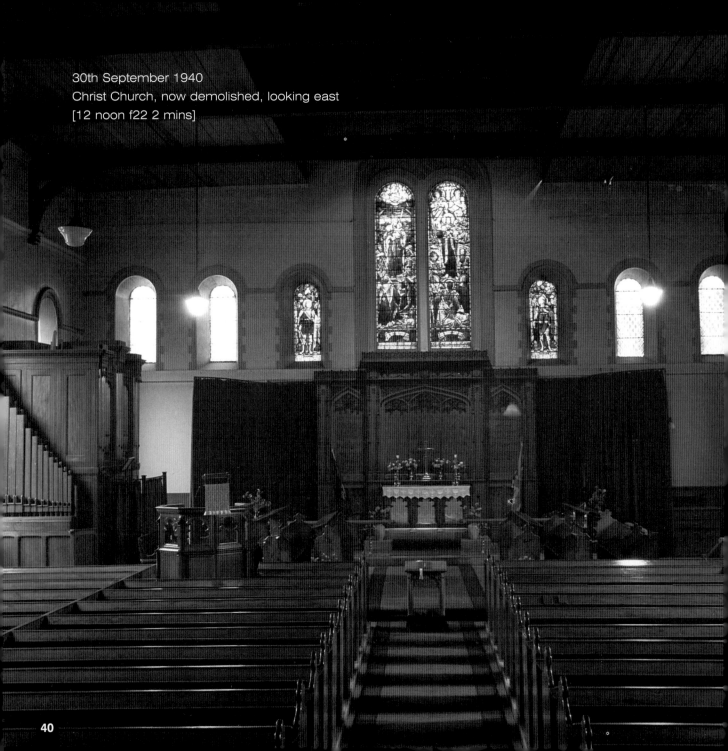

30th September 1940
Christ Church, now demolished, looking east
[12 noon f22 2 mins]

30th September 1940
Christ Church, altar from the south aisle
[12 noon f22 2 mins]

1935
St. James Young Men's Society Cricket team.
Front row second from left, Reg Hind;
back row from the right, David Horry, Kenneth Hind & Alan Whiteside

15th June 1940
The summer of the 'phoney war'. Whitehaven Secondary School XI,
Headmaster Mr.Burnett, Rex Malden played wicket keeper.
[4pm f5.6 $\frac{1}{100}$]

1936
The Cubs with their flag and totem.
The black armbands show mourning for King George V.

1936

The Scouts

August 1938
Scout Camp at Sleathwaite Farm
[12 noon f8 $^{1}/_{50}$]

August 1938
Scouts peeling
potatoes
[12 noon f8 $1/100$]

18th April 1938
Scouts at Haile, round the cooking fire
[4.30pm f11 1/25]

18th April 1938
George Porthouse
cutting bread to
make a sandwich
in the tent
[4.30pm f11 $1/25$]

18th April 1938
Joe Wilson & Fish Williamson at the campfire
[4.30pm f11 1/25]

August 1938
Round the campfire at Sleathwaite, Eskdale
[10pm f3.5 &* time] No flash light

18th April 1938
Scout camp at Haile
[4.30pm f11 ¹/₂₅]

15th March 1936
The Presentation
outside St. James'
Church hall by
John Shepherd to
Arthur Walker,
Scoutmaster of the
4th Whitehaven
(St. James) Scouts
& Cubs.

3rd June 1939
The wedding of
Arthur Walker &
Jean Nichol at
St. Saviours
Church, West
Hampstead

3rd June 1939
Cutting the cake.
Arthur Walker
became a Flight
Lieutenant in the
R.A.F. and was
killed on active
service on 17th
December 1943
leaving a widow,
and young son.

1936

The 6th Whitehaven Guides

Left to right Ruth Fitzgerald, Millicent Ferguson,
Edith McIntyre, Muriel Wilson & Sarah Scott

1936
Back row: Mr. Walker, Scoutmaster on left, next to Geoff Hall.
Front row: Margaret Williamson, Jean Nichol & Dolly Tweddle.

11th September 1940
My sister Anne taking the Brownie
oath beside the Toadstool in
St. James' Church hall

11th September 1940
The Brownies round their Toadstool

May 1939
Digging for worms
[4pm f11 $^1/_{50}$]

22nd July 1938
The Sunday School Trip to St. Bees beach
[5.30pm f8 $^{1}/_{100}$]

July 1939
'Wish we could go in'
[3.30pm f8 $^{1}/_{100}$]

St James Church from the south

August 1938
The Choir boys' trip to Lake Coniston
[6pm f8 $^{1}/_{100}$]

26th March 1938
Tommy Baker, Choirboy
[2pm f8 $1/100$]

26th March 1938
Tommy Garroway, Choirboy.
The suit & coat would have
come from Collis's the
pawnbrokers, where formal
clothes for fast growing
boys could be bought and
then 'exchanged' for a
bigger size.
[2pm f8 $^{1}/_{100}$]

July 1939
Long & Small Flimby filling station, the location of a Sunday School outing.
The garage is still operating in 2001
[12 noon f12.5 1/25]

21st July 1939
Mrs Wilson &
Mrs Geddes
getting into
Swings, Long
& Small Flimby
[3pm f8 $1/100$]

21st July 1939
Joe Wilson &
Harry Crock
enjoy the swings
Long & Small
Flimby
[3pm f8 $^1/_{100}$]

21st July 1939
The Roundabout, Long & Small Flimby
[6pm f5.6 ¹/₁₀₀]

19th November
1938
The Martinmas
Fair: Rolling
Pennies
[9pm f3.5 ¹/₂₅]

19th November
1938
Martinmas Fair at
the Harbour Side
Motor Race Track
[9pm f3.5 ¹/₂₅]

19th November 1938
The Martinmas Fair. The showman attracts customers with a microphone but then stands quiet while Jack Dansie is shooting. The prizes on offer included budgerigars in cages
[9pm f3.5 ¹/₂₅]

19th November 1938
The Martinmas Fair: Rex Malden with his shooting prize
[10pm f3.5 $^{1}/_{10}$ – taken by Jack Dansie]

12th July 1938
The Orange Lodge
Procession in
Scotch Street. The
Parade included
Workington, Maryport &
Whitehaven Lodges.
[12 noon f11 ¹/₅₀]

12th July 1938
Orange Lodge
Procession in
Scotch Street
[12 noon f11 1/50]

12th July 1938 Orange Lodge Procession. The Workington Banner. A workman's hut and a red flag mark where the road has been excavated for repairs. [12 noon f11 1/50]

12th July 1938
Orange Lodge
Procession
[12 noon f11 $1/50$]

12th July 1938
The Orange Lodge Procession. The children's section
[12 noon f11 1/50]

8th January 1938
A rehearsal for
Dick Whittington
in the Queen's
Theatre
[10pm f4.5 1/10]

8th January 1938
The Dick Whittington dancers
[10pm f4.5 $^1/_{10}$]

8th January 1938
The Dick Whittington Girl Dancers
[10pm f3.5 1/10]

24th October 1938
The Hensingham Amateurs perform in 'Maid of the Mountains'
[f3.5 ¹/₁₀]

26th April 1938
The Whitehaven Amateurs – The Mikado in the Queen's Theatre
[f3.5 1/10]

15th September 1938
Keir's Garage, with a choice of brands of petrol
[3pm f8 $1/50$]

15th September 1938
Keir's Garage
[3pm f8 1/50]

31st August 1938
Morrison's first electric milk float driven by J. W. Ellwood. It replaced a horse drawn delivery cart.
[3.30pm f8 1/50]

March 1938
A strange new
sign, St.Bees
[11.45am f8 $1/100$]

21st September 1938
A Modern Avenue. The National Grid was soon to replace local supplies of electricity
[2.30pm f8 $^1/_{50}$]

July 1939
Wheelbarrow
Brow
[7pm f2.9 $^1/_{25}$]

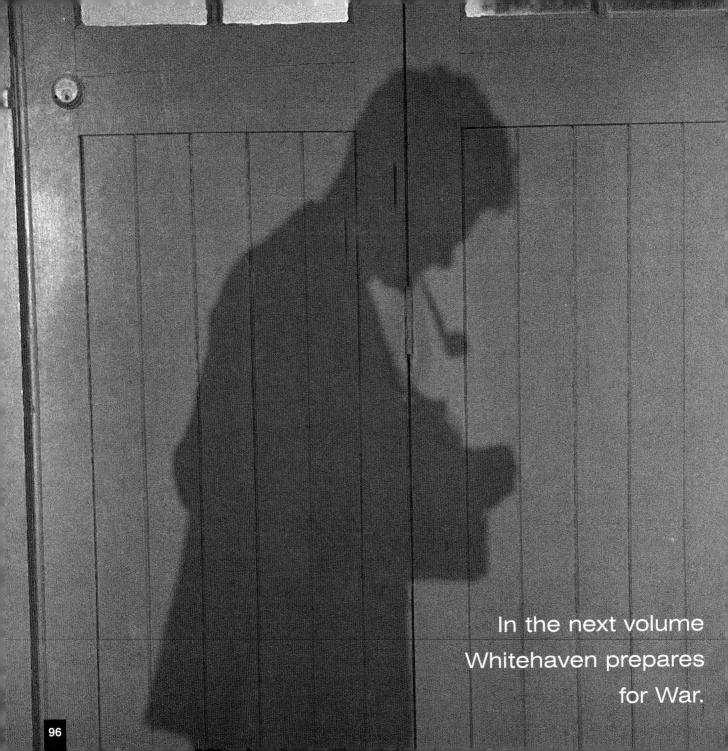

In the next volume
Whitehaven prepares
for War.